RISE UP

Other books by Victoria Reynolds

Transcending Fear

Own Your True Worth

Free Your Spirit

RISE UP

A Simplified Guide to
The Great Awakening,
Spiritual Revolution and
The Ascension

Victoria Reynolds

Rise Up: A Simplified Guide to the Great Awakening, Spiritual Revolution and The Ascension

Copyright 2020 © by Victoria Reynolds

No part of this may be used or reproduced by any means, graphic, electronic, or mechanical, including photocopying, recording, taping, or by any information-retrieval system, without the written permission of the publisher or author except in the case of brief, cited quotations embodied in critical articles and reviews.

The intent of this author is to offer information of a general nature to assist you in your quest for enhanced well-being and spiritual enlightenment. As personal transformation is an individual process, the author makes no guarantee or promises. The information provided within these pages is based on the author's personal insights.

Because of the dynamic nature of the Internet, any web addresses or links contained in this book may have changed since publication and may no longer be valid.

Updated November 2022

Freestyle Press
Hermosa Beach, CA 90254

ISBN: 978-1-954250-06-2(sb)
ISBN: 978-1-954250-02-4 (ebk)

Cover Design by Chelsey Marie Clark

"Hold your light so high that others can't help but see their own light"

—Victoria

Table of Contents

Introduction	1
What is The Great Awakening?	4
Why a Spiritual Revolution?	13
When is The Ascension?	23
Key Terms and Phrases	30
Bridging the Divide	100
Light Speed Ahead	105
The Returns	112
All for One	130
About the Author	140

"Picking sides always prevents you from finding a center."

—J.P. Sears

Introduction

In 2008, I began my personal great awakening and higher journey of ascension. It brought me home to who I am here to be. Throughout my life I've had many awakenings, aha moments that caused me to rethink everything I thought I knew. Each small awakening lead to greater understanding and seeing what I could not see before. My greatest awakening caused massive change in every aspect of my life: physical, emotional, mental, and spiritual. It led to my ability to see the full scope of what is happening on our planet, sometimes years in advance, and understand how the human experience has the potential to be joyful beyond our wildest imagination.

My own evolution, from growing up rooted in fear in an extremely fundamentalist religion to becoming an atheist to eventually discovering my own spiritual path, has allowed me to view this amazing time in our human experience from an expanded perspective that few others have.

In the pages of this simple guidebook, I share my understanding of our collective past and present, along with insights about moving forward as we work together to move out of a reality based on fear, control, and scarcity and into a new reality based on love, freedom, and prosperity for all.

I've also included terms and phrases I have found helpful in my own awakening process as well as what I've been seeing in the collective human process. Hopefully, the information I share here will give you an increased awareness of where we are heading and why it's such an exciting and important time to be alive.

"Where there is great doubt, there will be great awakening, small doubt, small awakening, no doubt, no awakening."

—Zen Proverb

What is The Great Awakening?

The Great Awakening is a time foretold across every culture and system of belief. It has been prophesied by many mystics, prophets, and visionaries. It has been long awaited by billions of people over thousands of years, each simultaneously hoping and fearing that the great unfoldment would take place during their lifetime.

This age marks the end of the known world when darkness breaks loose from the human story and light prevails. It is the time when all truths are revealed, secrets can no longer be kept, and deception is exposed. It is the time when all corruption is unveiled; the curtain is pulled away so humanity can see what was not visible before. It is the time when one season concludes, and a new season of humankind begins. It is a time when the entire hidden story is told, and people can no longer deny where they have been led astray. It is illuminating the deception and control that has been hidden in plain sight for eons, while also revealing the hidden successes and wins, as they did not fit into the fear-based agenda of the past. This glorious time is when all systems are crumbling, and new concepts are built to replace them.

This Great Awakening is the great dawning of a new day for humanity as we begin to see our true potential in the light and love of God, in

His/Her/Its many names, in all things. It is waking up to the truth of creation. It is bringing up our collective suffering to be healed. It is the breakdown of all things that leads to the greatest breakthrough humanity has ever seen.

Throughout the Earth story, since the beginning of known history, we have experienced many mini-awakenings and ages of enlightenment. When times get too dark, people begin to awake, rise up and rebalance the playing field as much as they know how. There have always been minds open enough to lead the way and guide the people in their uprising. Awakenings and ages of enlightenment are always based upon the quest for peace and freedom out of the darkness which precedes it.

Never before, has there been an awakening to this degree. This is the greatest transformation our planet and her people have ever experienced in our known history. The entire planet, citizens of all countries, are now living, experiencing life, and communicating together as one humanity — no longer weeks, days, months, or years apart. We are all present, all experiencing the same awakening at the same time, in this now moment. While preceding empires have come and gone, never has the whole world been ruled by one group of people; never have all the masses they overrule assembled to topple them. The people of Earth are waking up and finding their true power.

This is where we presently stand. We are on the precipice of creating an entirely new reality for all life on Earth as human beings work together to take back our planet from the control of greed and fear.

This Great Awakening is a global awareness of the fear, greed and corruption that has spread darkness like cancer across the entire planet and through all our systems. At the same time, this is the Great Enlightenment, when all people are learning how to see a bigger picture and bring more light into every facet of life.

This has been a long, dark night for the soul of humanity. Having lost our way in the darkness, we now need to look at our collective painful past, at all our fear-based beliefs and constructs and accept that everything we thought to be real begins collapsing around us. Disbelieving what we've always believed can be painful. The death of the old ways can be terrifying for those who cannot see what is on the other side. Right now, we are in the breakdown that always occurs before the breakthrough; the dark before the dawn. Trust that we will awaken into something deeper, something more real and meaningful than we've ever experienced before. We will find a collective resolve to create an entirely new world. Now that we know better, we can do better.

I lovingly refer to this process as the "Collective Holy-Shift," a time when people are drawn in and connected to their spiritual nature and all-loving truth. This Holy-Shift is a transitional period for all beings and for the planet herself. The global breakdown occurring now may be painful and messy, yet it is necessary for us to realize our divine potential. Transitions are never easy, but the euphoria and beauty that results are often beyond words. When we collectively emerge from darkness, it will be a whole new world. This unified Holy-Shift will lead to planetary experience we all desire to experience. This is a world where spirits are free to soar with no strings attached, hearts are free to love without fear, minds are free to create without limitation and bodies are free of all disease.

We are awakening to a whole new purpose for being. As the darkness fades away into the night, we emerge into the light of living love. It is the dawning of an entirely new creation. We are in the shakeup part of the wakeup. The Holy Shift, the shitstorm, the circus, the show, the rickety roller-coaster, the dark tunnel, the cocoon, the breakdown before the breakthrough, the apocalypse—whatever metaphor we choose to call it. This is our collective transformation.

If it feels like all Hell breaking loose, that is because it is. This transition of our our collective consciousness is bringing all darkness up to the surface for us to get a good, long, hard look and decide what we want to do with it. We can't move into the new way of being until we resolve our mutual issues and clean up our collective clutter. This disclosure of the clutter has already begun and as humanity wakes up to the greatest lies ever told we will ensure history never repeats again. We will learn from our shadows and dissipate the darkness of our past and create the world anew.

Yes, WE—because nothing happens on our planet without our consent, even when the consent is unconscious and coerced. And WE are now working together to consciously create a new reality where no one is seen as less than another. We are all Divine embodiments, and we are remembering who we really are.

"...the only revolution that can work is the inner transformation of every human being."

—Stanislav Grof

Why a Spiritual Revolution?

By its very nature, the dark side has no long-term vision because it cannot see in the dark. It has continued to play the same game plans throughout the long human story, and we have finally started to wise up. History repeating itself serves the purpose of learning from those dark lessons (mistakes), so we don't replicate them again and again. As we look back through our human story it is apparent the lessons were never really learned. It's the same story with different players playing out on the same field. Until we learn those lessons, rather than simply bandaging and hiding our collective suffering, we are destined to repeat them.

While our collective of souls agreed to learn through the contrast of light and dark, it was intended to be a balance of both, as day follows night and night follows day. Seeds germinate in darkness and reach into the light. But darkness permeated the everything and took over the entire Earth playing field. Human beings forgot they are the source of light and fell into the trap of darkness and the belief that they must fight each other over scraps rather than seeing each other as family. For too many, their heart lights dimmed, and they lost their way in the darkness.

The way to defeat the dark side and bring more light into our collective experience is to stop pretending the suffering doesn't exist or refuse to look at it. In a sense, see no evil, hear no evil, speak no evil allowed the darkness (what some call evil) to spread like cancer across the field and seep into every nook and cranny of the human experience. We need to remove the bandages and quick fixes that hide the suffering caused by our past mistakes. It is time to shine a light into the darkness, be willing to look at all the unpleasantness, learn the lessons found in the darkest places and then restore the balance of light and dark. We cannot dissipate the shadows if are unable to acknowledge their existence. Together we will reignite our own light until there are only grey shadows behind us to remind us of where we have been and how far we have come.

This, return to light and love, is a spiritual revolution, another turn as life revolves into new understanding. All revolutions and uprisings have been spiritual revolutions at their core. Revolutions occur when those who have been oppressed are no longer willing to tolerate oppression. The human heart, the human spirit, cannot be squelched—it can only be repressed for so long before it yearns to break free. Humanity's current oppression has only lasted this long because control and domination have been painted as safety and security. But now, too many have woken up, seen how they've been played and refuse to continue as pawns in the dark game.

This awakening and awareness of the dark game, recognizing how we've been played by deception and control, is a call for a new kind of revolution. Collectively, as one humanity, we are taking back our planet and demanding the freedom that is rightfully ours. Movements all over the world have been rising up, digging in, and pushing forward. Movements such as the Occupy Movement, Arab Spring, #MeToo, Black Lives Matter, V-Day, Rise Up for Children, QAnon, Anti-Vaxxers, and many others have made it possible for many who have felt hurt, and felt they had no voice, to no longer quiver in fear.

More and more people's voices are being heard as we eradicate the barriers created to keep humanity small, contained and divided. While you may not agree with how these movements have been politicized and used for division against each other, we can all agree they have expanded the voices of those who once had no voice. Giving voice to the voiceless serves us all. It allows us to move out of victimization and into empowerment as we find the courage to stand up to the oppressors of old and find the freedom, we are all meant to experience.

All humans yearn to be free; free to create, to love, to be happy and to simply be. Freedom is a God-given human right. When that is held back and confiscated by those who deem themselves in power, the yearning to be free wells up in the human heart and begins to rise. Each uprising is fueled by a spiritual movement even when it does not look that way on the surface. Revolutions cause breakdowns. With every breakdown comes new spiritual understanding and breakthroughs that lead to new worlds.

At the surface, revolution looks like a revolt against the status quo and chaos, as the existing order is no longer tolerable to those who are uprising. Revolt is not the same as revolution. From the spiritual perspective, revolution is taking another turn, a step up the spiritual spiral of understanding. It is an evolution of the soul. The word "revolution" has been misinterpreted to mean revolting against. Yet, it really means to make new. To begin a new turn and direction around a center point. The spiritual revolution we are presently in is just that. We are in a collective up-leveling within the spiritual spiral.

Every person who has experienced their own spiritual awakening recognizes this evolutionary process on the planet right now, which has been growing exponentially since the early 1960s. For the first time in our human story, the entire planet is experiencing a spiritual revolution, all at once, as we move collectively into the next phase of spiritual understanding. This new awareness of love is bringing about a complete understanding of Oneness beyond all division of religious dogmas.

As we look at what appears to be crumbling around us, remember that this is what we are leaving behind. We are evolving into a whole new reality, a higher consciousness of human spirit. Hold on to that knowing.

The Earth and all her beings are experiencing a baptism of fire. We are all learning hard lessons as we face our collective unresolved issues and are forced to remedy them once and for all. This fire is burning off everything that does not serve us as we move up into a more celestial way of living. It is returning us to our true divine potential as we find love, peace, and heaven within ourselves, and create it for the entire planet.

Envision an Earth where peace and plentitude are real and no longer just a dream. Imagine a world where love, harmony, freedom, equality, and prosperity are the new normal. Yes, there are many who believe this is impossible, but when enough of us make this our resolve, our revolution, it will be so.

"There's always another level up. There's always another ascension. More grace, more light, more generosity, more compassion, more to shed, more to grow."

—Elizabeth Gilbert

When is The Ascension?

The Ascension has been foreseen by ancient prophets as a time when all of humanity will be lifted into new golden age of harmony and prosperity. Every culture has a story about the end time and the beginning of a new time. That new time is The Ascension.

Spiritual Ascension is rising in higher and higher levels of loving consciousness and brighter light within us. The higher we each raise our loving consciousness in every thought, feeling and action, the closer we come to finding heaven within ourselves. This heaven within ourselves is translated and expressed outward into the world around us where we lift each other up into a collective ascension. We can literally reach the point where all that we see in the world around us is love, and life wanting to express itself as love. In this consciousness, we co-create peace and paradise on our Earth home.

The foretold Great Ascension is a process rather than a single moment in time. The rapture isn't an event but the love we feel expand within our own hearts. In my understanding, the ascension began around 1963 when love began returning to the planet as a first wave of higher vibration consciousness. It was the dawning of the Age of Aquarius, when peace, love and harmony started to become our collective reality and a part of our open conversation. The darkness of the Vietnam War spurred the Hippie Movement and love found a way into the human experience through them and their music. As people began waking up to the darkness around them, the negativity of the Cabal stepped up their side of the game. As light began returning to the planet the darkness went on defense. President John F. Kennedy was assassinated for his plan to expose the Cabal/Deep State. That event marked the beginning of the end of the old regime. Although it doesn't look this way, the darkness always works on behalf of the light. Dark moments in time such as this stirs up and wakes up those who could not see before.

It is always darkest at dawn and the dawning has come. As more people have awakened to the dark game, and humanity becomes more enlightened, the darkness appears to have become even darker. In truth, it hasn't become darker, it is simply light enough for us to see the darkness. Like any sunrise, the brighter the light gets, the darker the shadows appear, until the light becomes so bright the shadows begin to dissipate until they eventually disappear. As the light rises any remaining darkness becomes recognizable and navigable rather than being all-encompassing around us.

The light is rising, and the shadows once hidden in the darkness are becoming more visible. As the constructs of the past are made evident, they begin to crumble under the weight of new awareness. For those who cannot yet see, everything appears to be crumbling around them, and that can be terrifying. Hold them in compassion as we all move through this time of great change together. Remember, everyone awakens and ascends in their own time and in alignment with their own soul's journey.

This crumbling of old fear-based empires, constructs and systems is best for humanity and is a part of dissipating what no longer serves us. We cannot ascend into a new reality based in love while dragging systems created in fear and darkness with us. In our new reality, we will be restructuring all our systems to reflect love and light, rather than fear and darkness.

The Ascension is now. We are in the midst of it and it is in the midst of us. Those of us who choose to be the change we wish to see in the world are serving as divine interventions. We are calling it forward and creating it with every thought, word, feeling and action. The Ascension is a reflection of us, of who we choose to be. When enough of us choose to create a world based in love, it will become our collective reality. When enough of us ascend within ourselves, we will all ascend together, into the utopia that calls to us. Love is the vehicle for Ascension and is the energy of all creation.

We as one humanity, are ascending out of the world driven by fear and survival and into a new reality based only on love.

"Any fool can know. The point is to understand."

— Albert Einstein

Key Terms and Phrases

144,000: The chosen ones who are sealed to lead the Ascension, as mentioned in the New Testament and across many ancient cultures. Those who are the first to become both informationally and spiritually awake have been chosen to lead the way for the whole of humanity to rise into higher consciousness and the New Earth based solely in love. These chosen ones are often referred to as Light Leaders and Light Warriors.

3D to 5D: Referring to dimensions or densities of consciousness and our ascension from the 3rd

spiritual dimension based in fear and control, through the 4th dimension of transformation and transmutation and into the 5th dimension of pure, absolute, unconditional love or what is commonly referred to as Heaven on Earth.

Activation: Non-invasive transmissions of energy from practitioner to client, group, or audience, helping the client to bridge their physical body with their soul for a more peaceful and spiritually guided life. Activations are often effective in assisting all of humanity, as well as Mother Earth, to rise to a new potential. We can also activate our own gifts through processing our unresolved issues and past beliefs; however, having a facilitator creates a much faster and smoother process. Activation in conjunction with personal processing leads to a higher perspective of the human experience.

Alchemical Transformation: The process of energetically changing from one form to another. Changing our mind, heart, body, and aura to be more energetically aligned with higher vibrations of Spirit (AKA God), allowing us to become "light bodies" as the light within us grows and expands beyond the previous limitations caused by fear.

Apocalypse: From its Greek origins, this word means "revelation"—to uncover or reveal what was not known before the unveiling. It has been mis-interpreted to mean the final destruction of the world. It is simply the end of the old world as we work together to create a new Earth. It is the end of the world for those being exposed for their dark deeds and the beginning of a new world for the rest of humanity.

Archangels: Angels of the highest rank. Their purpose is to guide and protect all humankind. They work very closely with the Ascended Masters to ensure humanity's progress.

Ascended Masters: Beings who once lived on Earth in physical form. They mastered the human experience and as evolved souls, now have committed themselves to helping humanity navigate the Earth experience. They are dedicated to protecting human evolution and Earth's Ascension. They are also often referred to as angels and the angelic realm.

Aura: An energy field surrounding each of us that is emitted from the heart. It is also referred to as our spiritual body. The lighter and more loving our heart, the more powerful our auric field is in its ability to transmute approaching fear and attract into our lives a more loving and spiritual Earth experience.

Awakened/Awakening: No longer moving through life unconsciously. Awakening is multi-faceted: mental, emotional, physical, and spiritual. All awakenings lead to greater freedom. When individuals wake up, they find greater personal freedom—as that freedom spreads outward, it leads to collective freedom. Some people are more awake and able to see what has been hidden and disguised in our physical world, while others are more awake and able to see what has been hidden in our spiritual world. Once those who are awake to physical disclosure come together with those who are awake to spiritual disclosure, they will become a light force that cannot be stopped.

Beings of Light: Non-physical beings on Earth and in our air space who are here to assist us and protect us from harm. These include Guardian Angels, Spirit Guides, Ascended Masters, Archangels, Benevolent ETs, and Elohim.

BLM/ANTIFA: Movements against racism, fascism, corporatism, and other "isms" that limit human equality and keep those at the bottom small. Some people speculate these primarily peaceful protestors have been infiltrated and funded by individuals with nefarious agendas to instigate chaos and violence while also funding police aggression toward protestors. Funding both sides ensures greater hatred and division among people, prevents humanity from coming together in unity, and ensures those at the top of national and global systems retain their present positions of control.

Cabal: Ancient ruling bloodlines who see it as their divine right to control all of humanity and every aspect of the human experience. Working with dark forces, they use fear tactics, arcane symbology, and other tools to retain control. They were formerly known as Illuminati until more people caught on and started exposing their secrets. Over the millennia, they have often rebranded to keep themselves and their dark agenda hidden. To confuse the masses, they choose names that stand for the opposite of what they really represent; for example, Illuminati indicates being enlightened, but they are false light. As Zionists, they mis-identified themselves as Jewish, but they are not. They are the global leaders of the dark side and work diligently to maintain their agenda and purpose of control. Cabal was also a term used in Nazi Germany as a label for all Jews to drive antisemitism and is currently recognized as an antisemitic term.

Chakras: Energy centers in the body that help people stay balanced and connected to both Earth and Heaven. The more we clear our chakras of mental, emotional, and spiritual clutter, the more connected we can be to Divinity, with an easier flow of inspired energy.

Channeling: Receiving communication and messages from Spirit. Each of us is a stream of consciousness connected to the All That Is, which many call "God." We each have the capacity to "tune in" to higher guidance from higher levels of consciousness that we can access by going inward (and upward). As we raise our own internal vibration into greater loving within ourselves, we can receive higher vibration messages in the same way the prophets of old once did. Channeling is the modern term for receiving revelation.

Christ Consciousness: The consciousness of unconditional love, pure heart of a child and oneness with the Creator. Because Jesus of Nazareth, also known as Yeshua ben Joseph, exemplified this consciousness more than any other being on Earth, he was given the title of Christ. Those in greatest awareness of Spirit strive to hold this degree of loving consciousness within themselves. As more people experience an awakening, the more Christ Consciousness will flood the planet.

Clearing: The process of releasing, letting go and discharging mental, emotional, physical, and spiritual clutter within one's auric field so that all that remains is a clear path, purpose, and connection to the Divine. Clearing can also apply to cleaning up and decluttering one's physical space to create a calmer existence.

Cognitive Dissonance: The state of holding conflicting beliefs. This can cause a complete stalemate and standstill in personal and collective progress as the conflicting beliefs attempt to cancel each other out. Therefore, conscious discernment is key. Processing old, limiting beliefs allows us to move forward into new, more empowering beliefs as we let go of those that block our full divine potential.

<u>Collective Consciousness</u>: The combined beliefs of any given group, society, or culture. Every thought, belief, perception, and action each of us experiences are energy; this unites with a larger field of energy that flows through all things as we each feed into it and it streams into us. When enough people focus in one direction, even when the actions are not obvious, others become affected by those thoughts. In fact, it is impossible for our thoughts and actions not to affect every other being on Earth. Note this is not the same as hive mind which can be used to manipulate groups of individuals or the human collective. Collective consciousness requires we are conscious of the thoughts and beliefs and use this consciousness with intent for the highest and greatest good of the whole.

Collective Reality: The combined reality for all life on Earth. Conscious communication between individuals, where two or more are gathered in agreement, disrupts patterns in the old reality and begins new forward actions, which then become the new reality for those individuals. These also feed into the airwaves where we all unconsciously become affected by each other's thoughts. When enough people think in a particular direction, it creates action toward that direction, and that becomes our collective reality. If we want to create change, it requires a critical mass to place focused intent in that direction.

Conscious: The state of being awake and aware.

Conscious Choice: Deliberate and mindful choosing. Whether we recognize it or not, most of our choices are made unconsciously; or rather, by our subconscious thoughts, which are based on subconscious beliefs. Most of our choices are made without really thinking about them. Once we recognize the difference between conscious living and unconscious programming, we can choose deliberately to make changes in our personal and collective world.

<u>Conscious Objective Observer</u>: One who has the capacity to look at a situation without becoming emotionally charged and the ability to recognize how to best discharge the dark forces and negative energies within that situation. Observing without getting sucked into the emotional charge is essential for inner peace and seeing clearly what is necessary to move forward. While the full range of emotions is a unique part of the human experience, our ability

to feel and then hold in neutrality is part of the human mastery.

Conspiracy Theories: All beliefs or concepts identifying individuals and/or corporations to have conspired against the wellbeing of a group, culture, or humanity at large. Some are mindless theories which cannot be substantiated and can be harmful. Some are conspiracy fact which can be substantiated but the substantiation has not been released openly to the public. As theories become proven facts, they become part of history, although quite often without public acknowledgement. The government testing the effects of LSD on unwitting US and Canadian citizens is an example of a conspiracy theory becoming conspiracy fact yet swept under the rug for the unwitting masses.

Dark Overlord: Also referred to as Satan, Lucifer, Beelzebub, Devil, and other names that represent the purveyor of fear, deception, and temptation. This non-physical entity is represented in many different depictions and exists for the sole purpose of propagating the fear and darkness many call evil. He has numerous minions of varying authority levels working in every system on Earth until we cleanse the planet of him and his deeds. The Earth will then be restored to a place of peace and become the garden it was before fear arrived here.

Dark Side: The dark contrast in the human experience. As souls, we agreed to experience the contrast of the Earth school and accepted the challenge of finding our own light in the darkness. For us to experience this contrast, there is a dark side in all things, even within ourselves. The darkness is meant for us to learn through and not to be consumed by. When our souls collectively choose for Earth to be a resting place, the dark side will cease to exist, and fear will simply become a medium for growth.

Dark to Light: Restoring the balance of contrast. Fear and darkness have been spreading over our planet like a virus to the human heart and mind. As more people have been finding their own light, the darkness has become darker. The Great Awakening is exposing the darkness, shining a light upon it, and dissipating it until all that remains are shadows of our past to process and learn from.

Deception: Fear disguised as love and darkness disguised as light. The dark side has always known how to deceive the human mind into acting in ways that cause harm against ourselves and others, believing we are doing it for the light. Discernment is the key to staying above the fray and deciphering whether what we are being told is the truth of love and light, or a deception painted as such.

Deep-State/Globalists: An undefined group of individuals and their multi-layered corporations that manipulate and control every aspect of the collective human experience and give the illusion that we have free-will-choice through blind compliance. This web controls religion, government, and financial institutions as well as all most media, food production, medicine and nearly every way of life. They control humanity from the belief that they possess superior minds and capabilities, and the masses are incapable of choosing what is best for them. In this belief, they have corrupted the entire human experience and broken the prime directive of free-will-choice.

Digital Warriors: Individuals who recognize that we are in a revolution and doing what is necessary to help expose the darkness and free humanity from its hold. They are a rebel alliance working across the globe to spread the truth. They use all social media sites to send the messages forward, very much like other underground communications in previous revolutions and uprisings yet utilizing the newest technologies.

Dimensions: Spiritual (rather than physical) dimensions of consciousness. The higher we raise our personal consciousness into greater loving and higher light, the more we move into higher dimensions of living and being. Collectively, we have all been living in a third-dimension reality where we have experienced and learned through the polarity of fear and love. The fourth dimension converged with the third dimension in 2012 and is the reason we have been experiencing the extreme duality. The fourth dimension is driven by emotion. It is the veil between heaven and Earth. It is called the dark tunnel, limbo, spiritual prison, breakdown, cocoon, dark night of the soul and other names for the darkness of transformation before exiting into the fifth dimension. The fifth dimension is where our minds, hearts, bodies, and spirits exist only in love, prosperity, and harmony with each other and all beings. The fifth dimension is the Ascension destination. Higher dimensions are available for consciousness and energetic co-creation.

Disclosure: Exposing mass corruption and deception. Corruption is being brought into the open and put out into full view for all the world to acknowledge and notice where humanity has been manipulated. Disclosure is the first step to healing. It is necessary to learn the lessons that need to be learned from the experience and create a new world where the corruption cannot be duplicated. Disclosure is also used as a term for exposing the existence of off-planet beings as governments admit their existence.

Disinformation Warfare: Deliberate mistaken information provided to the public through mainstream and social media outlets. The disinformation campaign exists across every issue, and on both sides of every issue, to confuse, mislead and divide the masses.

<u>Divine Human Blueprint</u>: Original genetic design for the human species. This blueprint was pure, free of disease and corruption and had the capacity for magical manifestation. It was coded for love, compassion, and prosperity. Once fear infiltrated our planet, as described in many of our ancient myths like the Garden of Eden, our genetic makeup became corrupted. This created disconnection, lack and competition. We are now striving to restore our original genetic code and blueprint where all things become possible as love through us.

<u>Divine Intervention</u>: Direct assistance of God, angels, benevolent extraterrestrials, and beings of light. As creators and embodiments of God,

we are also divine intervention in action as we work together to create a new reality based in love.

Dogma: An inflexible set of principles, rules, or beliefs. It is the groundwork of many religions and can also be an ideology of any kind where "my way is the only way." It can be so ingrained that it becomes part of an individual's personal identity. This can often lead to being so blinded by belief they simply cannot see the perspective of anyone else.

Empowerment: Power from within. Finding our true divine human potential within ourselves and using our divine power to help heal and transform the world.

Enlightenment: Greater understanding of possibility. The mind becomes open to allow more creative light to enter and as this happens, we can see new possibilities for ourselves and all life on Earth. More light, love, beauty, creativity and even a greater spectrum of color stream through new levels of light and love consciousness.

Extraterrestrials: Beings that are not of human form or of Earth's origins. Many people now acknowledge that we are not alone in the Universe and that the entire Universe was not created just to support humans. ETs have been spoken and written about since the beginning of known time. These non-human life forms can be either benevolent or malicious. Angels and demons might also be included among them, as mentioned in some ancient texts. Some exist in our airspace and share Earth space with us in dimensions we simply cannot see.

Fake News: News that is distorted to meet a particular agenda or is entirely untrue. In a world where anyone can say anything without having real proof, can twist or alter facts or manipulate with green screens, fake footage and photoshopping, it has become vital that we use discernment to determine if a story is true or not. We are past the Information Age and well into the present Age of Discernment, which means developing our conscious choice muscle and learning how to listen to our inner guidance, the only real voice of truth.

Fear: False Evidence Appearing Real. At its core, fear is our basic response to stress and is instinctual to basic survival. However, for some people in our human story it became a tool for control and manipulation. Fear provides us with opportunities for growth and learning through the darkness; however, holding onto fear-based beliefs prevents us from moving forward and finding our true divine potential within the human experience.

Fear-Based Beliefs: Individual and collective beliefs that keep human beings small-minded, limited, divided, and controlled. These beliefs stifle the human spirit and prevent us from creating to our full potential. Fear-based beliefs create judgement and division between each other, and separation from God.

Fiat Money System: The monetary system connected to the Federal Reserve, Internal Revenue Service, International Monetary System and the banking industry. This configuration is based entirely on debt and borrowing money that pays interest. Our birth certificates and social security numbers are used to borrow against us. We are the collateral that backs our currency rather than gold-backed currency. It is also referred to as the enslavement system since it is driven by human productivity. Productive taxpayers are recognized and seen as assets while unproductive members of society are considered liabilities by those who control the system.

Focused Intent: Where we maintain our thoughts, attention, and intention. Our thoughts are just as, or even more, powerful as our actions. Thoughts, if held long enough, become our beliefs, and beliefs lead to actions. Our attention and intention—how and where we place our focused thoughts—drive the creation of our reality.

Foundations: Non-profit trusts that exist for humanitarian and environmental benefit. They are primarily accessible to the ultra-rich and are often used as a means of paying less taxes than would be paid otherwise. In the hands of the dark side, they are used for money laundering and nefarious activities, while giving the impression they are working for light. That is what the dark side does, using words that appear light and loving to obfuscate that their intentions are the opposite of that name. This tactic deliberately makes it difficult for humanity to decipher light from dark or love from fear; effectively hides the deception; and ensures the successful infiltration of all systems without detection.

Frequencies: Everything in existence vibrates as energy. Thoughts have frequency. The heart emits electronic frequency. The planet has its own frequency. Lower frequencies are based in fear and higher frequencies are based in love. Lower, fear-based frequencies are dark, heavy, oppressive, limiting and sabotaging. Wallowing in them can lead to dis-ease of the mind, body, heart, and spirit. Higher, love-based frequencies are light, uplifting, supportive, expressive, expansive, and empowering. Swimming in them makes all things possible.

Galactic Federation: Off world beings who have agreed to assist humanity and the Earth through its ascension process. As of 2022 those who work on the side of light have asked to be referred to as The Light Alliance as some members of The

Galactic Federation have been tempted to switch sides and now work for the dark side.

GCR: Global Currency Reset. The envisioned future balance of money and restoration of all currencies across the planet to full value based on each country's natural resources. This may also include total debt forgiveness between countries so that all countries start with fresh balance sheets and may include redistribution of wealth back to the people. This would be a transition phase, as the New Earth based in love and harmony may have no physical form of exchange, only giving and receiving from the heart, and cooperation in all things.

Global Financial Reset: A rebalancing of the books. The goal is to end our present debt-based currencies as Reserve systems are closed out and new money becomes backed by natural resources rather than human resources. Money will be exchanged through a new Quantum Financial System, (not the same as digital currency), allowing for free flow throughout the globe. This reset will lead to more personal freedoms, religious freedoms, economic freedoms, and political freedoms as humanity is no longer bound by financial enslavement.

Great Reset: Not to be confused with Global Financial Reset. Many say this is the globalist vision of further enslaving and controlling humanity. It is part of the New World Order 2030 Agenda now in process, with a goal of eventually being able to track, manage and control all life on Earth. On the surface it looks like the answer to all our problems. It proposes financial security, job security, free education, free housing, and complete debt forgiveness, all in exchange for higher taxes and less personal freedoms. It leads to total global control.

Golden Age: The time of peace, freedom, and prosperity for all life on Earth. Some predict it will last for over 1,000 years. Others say humanity will be invited to become part of the Galactic Federation as we become advanced enough to understand higher protocols and teach other planets what we have learned.

Higher Consciousness: Being spiritually awake and attuned to higher knowing. It is internalizing the awareness of our direct connection to the unseen, our higher-self, higher-mind, and infinite connection to Source/God/All That Is.

Humanitarianism: Belief in the value of human life and in actively assisting other humans to improve conditions of humanity and all life on Earth. This is an activation of the humanitarian heart where the focus of life becomes service to the highest and greatest good of all concerned rather than service to self

Illuminate: To light up the darkness in order to see our personal and collective shadows, learn more from them and de-energize their unconscious power to create division and keep us from our full divine potential.

Infiltration: Dark hijacking and control of minds, organizations, and systems, often without awareness of those being infiltrated. Our minds are connected to a stream of consciousness through multiple dimensions, all the way up to the highest divine, loving truth of God. This is how we become inspired to create and imagine in the likeness of God. If we do not protect our minds, the stream of consciousness can be hijacked by lower energies, as dark, negative, and fear-based thoughts. This hijacking causes us to think, act, speak and act in unloving, hurtful ways toward each other. Every person who has ever performed acts of so-called evil or harmed another being has been infiltrated by negative influences. Prayer, meditation, and specific intention can create spiritual protection from infiltration. Infiltration of organizations and systems can also occur as individuals with ill intent make their way into decision making positions and turning a well-meaning organization into a nefarious one without supporter's awareness of the change.

Inner Work: Digging into our past beliefs, painful memories, traumas, and unresolved issues to heal, resolve, let go and discharge everything that does not serve our highest good and blocks us from being in Divine flow. This is based on the understanding that wherever we go we take ourselves with us. If we are to be the change in the world, we must first be willing to change ourselves; to dive deep into our psyches to heal all that needs to be healed and resolve all that needs to be resolved. We do this to serve as a beneficial presence on Earth.

Light Workers: Individuals across the planet who have found their own light and are working to grow the light consciousness. They can be found in every belief system and community around the world, as shining beacons for humanity. These people became spiritually awakened and activated their spiritual gifts before most others to help the masses emotionally and spiritually navigate the Great Awakening and Collective Holy Shift, while also facilitating the required healing to move forward into the higher consciousness of Ascension. They lovingly support all systems of belief, knowing every person has their own path to God, and often have a direct connection with God. Some are also referred to as Light Leaders and Light Warriors.

Magic/Witchcraft/Sorcery: Working with energy to create a desired result. Magic itself is neither good nor evil; however, the way it is used and who it is used by determines whether it is light magic or dark magic. We live in a magical universe. The Universe works its magic through human choice and synchronicity. Those who work with dark magic are only more effective because those who work in the light have been told to fear magic. Light is more powerful than dark, and we need only learn how to wield it more effectively.

Mainstream Media/MSM: Corporate syndicated, nationwide, and multi-national outlets assumed by the masses to be the only source for truth. Mainstream media has always been used by governments and regimes as propaganda for control and to program the masses through fear-based news. Every revolution and liberation that has ever been won on behalf of the people, resulted through underground movements and independent communication. This is now often referred to as alternative media.

Master Mind: The All Mind of the universe, Source/God from which all creation flows. Each of us has the capacity to tune in and receive divine guidance from the Master Mind.

Mockingbird Media: The multitude of MSM news outlets repeating the same talking points and reading the same scripts on camera. It is a very efficient and effective form of propaganda for social programming and subconscious brainwashing. This modern term may directly relate to Operation Mockingbird from the 1970s.

Multi-Dimensional: The consciousness of experiencing life and circumstances through more than one spiritual dimension. Multi-dimensional consciousness is part of the human expansion. Although we live in the physicality of Earth, which is presently based in fear, our consciousness has the capacity to communicate with higher dimensional beings and experience our reality in higher dimensions of thought. Through multi-dimensional consciousness, we can bring heaven to Earth.

Narrative: Predetermined plots and storylines to maneuver humanity in a particular direction.

Negative Influences: Unseen deception and dark infiltration. Negative influences exist in all systems and are so pervasive they can keep us mentally and spiritually asleep and blind to the bigger picture playing out on our planet.

New Age: The current era of enlightenment. Combines new spiritual understanding with ancient wisdom. Tools and healing modalities once used in ancient times have been restored with a deep love for Spirit. Many who don't understand this as a deeply loving and divine light practice have been taught to be afraid of it. Some have been taught that new enlightenment is evil when it is quite the opposite. This misperception is another deception fed to humanity to maintain fear, keep us divided and prevent us from finding more love, light, freedom, and spiritual connection. There are a few members in the New Age of Enlightenment community who have been mistakenly swayed into a movement driven by false light.

New Earth: What the planet will become once we rise up and out of our present fear-based reality and create an entirely new reality based solely in love. This New Earth is akin to the Garden of Eden—a symbol of what Earth was before fear was introduced to the planet. We left our Mother's garden to experience right/wrong perspectives and learn from our experiences through the contrast of fear. We are returning to the garden where all of life flourishes and we will once again be at peace.

NESARA/GESARA: The National/Global Economic Security and Recovery Act, a proposal and plan suggested by Harvey Francis Barnard to establish harmony, equality and prosperity for humanity and remove corruption from all systems. Some say the Act has been approved and is in the process of being enacted.

One Earth Consciousness: Understanding that we are all one family and that our planet is home for every one of us equally. This consciousness is based solely in love, caring and compassion. Because all beings are created equal and are equally worthy of love and thriving, we take care of each other, all life forms, and the Earth by loving choice.

One World Order/New World Order: A devised plan for the Cabal/Elite/Powers-that-Be—those who see themselves as above the rest of humanity—to take over every world system and remove personal freedom. It is a plan of absolute control in the disguise of security and absolute power in the disguise of safety. Their plan is one global government, with all banking, currency, taxes, healthcare, agriculture, food, education, and environment all managed under one system, with those at the top making choices for all the rest, who feed into the system through human production. Simply put, it is a slave and master system, with the slaves treated well enough that they don't revolt. This is global totalitarianism.

On the surface, it is sold to us in a way that looks much like One Earth Consciousness, which is why so many people unconsciously support it; but it is a deception. They are mirror images of each other, one on the light side and the other on the dark side, and they lead to opposite realities.

Oneness: The understanding that we as humanity are all one body of consciousness and we are all one with God. As such, it is impossible to be separate from each other. All choices we make—individually, as co-creators with God and as inter-creators with each other—affect all life on Earth and become our collective reality.

Patriots: Individuals who are sworn to uphold the original constitutions of their free countries and are committed to the freedom of humanity and all life on Earth. Many also consider themselves to be revolutionaries and rebels against the tyranny of One World Order. The dark side uses mainstream media to portray Patriots as gun-loving, racist, misogynistic, anarchist, far right-wing, lunatic conspiracy theorists, while most are simply in the online trenches fighting for the freedom and protection of all humanity.

Pattern Interrupt: This occurs when breaking an individual's routine, habitual thoughts or behavioral patterns in a deliberate way that shakes them up. Being shaken out of our habitual patterns is part of the awakening process. The COVID-19 coronavirus is an example of a mass pattern interrupt, giving all of humanity an opportunity to wake up and begin a collective quantum leap of consciousness and global transformation. Both the virus and the so-called vaccine that followed are prime examples of how the darkness exists to serve the light.

<u>Personal Shadows:</u> Aspects of us that are based in fear and judgment. Everything and everyone on our planet are made of aspects that are both light and dark. It is the contrast our souls agreed to navigate in order to find true light within ourselves and return to the light of God within. All beings show their good side, their light side, on the surface. The shadows are kept in the dark. These shadows are the subconscious controllers of our reality until we expose them by illuminating our inner light and turning to face them. These shadows are fear-based beliefs and aspects of ourselves that we have ignored and even shunned, which continue to control us until we face, recognize, heal, and transmute them with love. If not acknowledged, processed, and

resolved, they become darker and deeper, leading to painful relationships and dis-ease in the mind, heart, and body. There are also collective shadows in our human story that need to be healed.

Prime Directive: The primary law under which all other laws follow. The prime directive for Earth is free-will-choice. This is the primary law of God for our planet and cannot be broken or interfered with. Those who have been intentionally tampering with free-will-choice will be brought to justice during the Great Awakening process.

Processing: The act of intentionally looking at all of one's unresolved issues, painful experiences, and past beliefs with the objective of consciously learning from them. Learning takes place by determining whether each belief and memory is based in fear or love; if they are based in fear, you must change your perspective and perception by reframing them, so that they become beneficial to your personal and spiritual growth.

Project Looking Glass: Advanced technology said to be owned by the U.S. military allowing individuals to see into the future to view all potential outcomes. This secret project was leaked to the public in early 2020. It is hypothesized that this technology came from reverse-engineering crashed extraterrestrial spaceships. My personal understanding is that it works by computing all timeline options and alternate realities related to the end game, providing the "good guys" with the ability to navigate each play so that every possible scenario ends with the Light winning on behalf of humankind. It is akin to a very complex game of chess, requiring forethought of every possible move made by both the Light and dark sides, with each side playing out their moves for the intended final result before leading into the next phase of human evolution.

Projecting: Making judgments about another person's character based on unconscious beliefs one has about themselves. Inner unconscious negative beliefs and judgments we have about ourselves, and past experiences become the lens through which we view other people, whether they have those same qualities. Projections of self-judgment prevent us from seeing divinity in ourselves and others. This projection process also occurs with positive beliefs, as we assume others hold themselves to the same standards we hold for ourselves.

Q/QAnon: Q is an enigma, a series of codes for deciphering and communicating The Plan for exposing corruption and bringing justice for all. Some hypothesize that Q is an individual or military intelligence with access to Project Looking Glass. Others speculate it is an Artificial Intelligence. QAnon are followers of Q and decode the messages of the plan. Members of QAnon are global allies who dig into the tunnels of corruption, decipher the Q codes, then spread the decoded messages forward to what are recognized as revolutionaries and awakening ones. Contrary to many media outlets, Q and those who associate as QAnon are not all far-right or members of a radical cult. This is a movement of primarily peaceful truth seekers in the center of the political divide, many who prefer not to be labeled as liberal or conservative.

Quantum Leap: A rapid advance in evolution. Evolution is a process that takes place over long periods of time, adapting to change as needed for survival and expansion. Occasionally, there is a leap in consciousness, often ignited by those we might call our greatest Masters in science, technology, art, music, spirituality, and other areas, rather than the slow, consistent growth of physical evolution.

Red Pill: Accessing hidden information (derived from the 1999 science-fiction film, The Matrix). Someone has been "red-pilled" when they start seeing the disclosure of hidden truth and misinformation fed to them by the mainstream media and recognizing the false reality they've been living in. Being red-pilled can be extremely uncomfortable as it causes initial cognitive dissonance before the truth settles in.

Reflecting/Mirroring: Having our own issues and qualities being mirrored back to us by another person or situation. Who we are and what we believe about ourselves—both positive (inner light and love) and negative (our dark shadows) is reflected back to us to see it inside ourselves for self-awareness and healing.

Resurrection: Lifting and restoring our wholeness and the wholeness of The Divine in all things. This includes resurrecting the Divine Feminine with all Her goodness, compassion, caring, understanding, and nurturing to heal the broken hearts of humanity and restore Her mantle alongside the Divine Masculine in unity and harmony.

RV: Revaluation of currencies. See GCR for more details.

Sacred Geometry: The symbology of geometric designs found throughout all of nature, presumed to be of divine origin. Such patterns can be found in every culture and belief systems, back to the beginning of known history.

Satanic Rituals: Practices performed to appease Satan and all lords of darkness. Satan is the overseer of darkness and is the god of false light. He has also been recognized as Lucifer, the fallen angel of light, along with other depictions throughout history. Following him presumably guarantees becoming a star—an eternal legend in the limelight with limitless wealth and notoriety. His guarantees, however, require human sacrifice, often cloaked in the guise of war or violence, while using God's name in vain as justification for harm against the bodies of humanity. Sacrifices are also performed in secret rituals, ensuring that one's soul is committed to the dark side. As we create a world based in love, all who worship the dark side and sacrifice humanity in exchange for greed will be exposed and removed from the Earth experience.

Second Coming: The return of Christ Consciousness. This return ensures we all ascend into a new reality of unconditional love, inner peace, mutual acceptance, and divine oneness. Some believe this Christ Consciousness has already returned to the planet and has been playing a vital role in the spiritual awakening of the masses, which has been in process since the 1960s. Others believe The Christ will return in physical form to lead the way into a New Earth reality and oversee the reconstruction of humanity.

Secret Societies: Groups and organizations whose activities, events, functions, or membership are concealed from non-members. Those currently thought to be connected to the Cabal/Deep State include: The Illuminati, The Freemasons, Skull and Bones and Bilderberg. Some also postulate that the Council on Foreign Relations and the United Nations, among many other organizations with a Humanitarian front are secretly working on behalf of the Cabal and the New World Order.

Shadow Government: Governing that takes place secretly, behind the scenes of what we see on the surface. The shadow government gives the impression of representing us, serving us protecting us, and making choices that are best for us. However, beneath the surface are individuals who control and steal from the masses, while painting it as "social security, welfare and safety." The shadow uses words to make us feel safe and secure, while siphoning the tax money we have entrusted to them for our collective well-being, instead using it to feed their greed and need for control.

Social Engineering: Intentional psychological manipulation of people to get them to act in a certain way in order to regulate the future development of a culture. This is most effective with repetitive media propaganda, particularly when also concurrent with heightened fear and driven by emotion. This may also include censoring information that does not align with the developmental goal.

Spirit Guides: Also referred to as guardian angels and passed loved ones. For some people, whose role it is to help guide humanity on the ground, this also includes planetary guardians and archangels. We all have the capacity to communicate with our guides telepathically. Many have simply been told they cannot (or should not) and have therefore never activated their telepathy beyond basic intuition.

Spiritual Alchemy: Spiritual transformation. See alchemical transformation for details.

<u>Spiritual Bypass</u>: Recognizing our personal and collective unresolved issues and declaring they no longer bother us because we have risen above them, without extracting the full lesson the suffering can provide and processing the emotional attachments to those stories. We then stuff the issues back down so that we no longer need to look at them, because we would rather focus only on what feels good. This is marginally better than the denial that sweeps emotional pain under the rug or puts it in a closet so we can pretend it never existed. However, until those issues are resolved and healed, they will continue to surface again and again, until they are fully healed and permanently learned from. We can recognize spiritual bypassing when there are still negative reactions surrounding a particular experience; it often goes hand-in-hand with spiritual arrogance and self-righteousness.

Spiritual Hijacking: The dark side using spiritual practices, tools, technologies, terms, and phrases for its own dark purposes. This sometimes makes it difficult for humanity to decipher light from dark, love from fear, as the dark side is a mirror image of light side.

Spiritual Progression: The evolution of the soul as it learns through life experiences. Many believe this occurs over multiple lifetimes, and possibly other planets, as continual learning until one achieves spiritual mastery.

Spiritual Protection: Shielding our mind, heart, body, and auric field, along with everything in our domain of care, from negative and nefarious energies. We all have the capacity to protect ourselves from infiltration of other people's thoughts, beliefs, feelings, projections, and energy as well as negative energy from anything outside of ourselves, including dark spells, magic, hijacking and tracking. Spiritual protection is especially vital for those who dig into dark tunnels of corruption. Digging into the darkness can attract spiritual leaches and dark entities into the mind, causing depression, anger, resentment, and extreme judgment in even the most loving person. Knowing our word is law, and we create our reality, we can claim protection of our mental, emotional, physical, and spiritual bodies.

Spiritual Tools: Metaphysical and physical techniques to help stay connected to peace, love, and Source (AKA God). These methods can include breathing to a calm center, gratitude, forgiveness, compassion, prayer, meditation and so on. Some people choose to use these in conjunction with physical tools such as sacred geometry, candles, crystals, incense, sacred emblems, and tokens such as a rosary or cross to help them stay spiritually grounded.

Spiritually Awakened: Enlightened and open to greater possibilities of our human nature and awakened to the divinity within ourselves and others.

St. Germain Trust: Also known as the World Trust Fund, it is based upon the Earth's abundance of precious metals and jewels. Although originally of good intent, the original flow through trusts and foundations have been compromised and are no longer pure of heart. If new and benevolent foundations can replace those previously chosen, then the St. Germain Trust may become enacted as once planned.

Star Seeds: highly advanced spiritual beings and souls originating from distant planets, other solar systems, and galaxies and have volunteered to assist humanity and the Earth through the Ascension process. Many are souls incarnated in human form.

Telepathic Communication: The ability to communicate non-verbally. Most people experience this in long-term relationships, for example in marriage, where they know what the other person is going to say in advance. Telepathy is the ability to hear what is not being said out loud. It is how we communicate with God and how God communicates with us. It is a form of communication that can be activated and practiced. Non-verbal autistics are often born with this gift fully activated and often have an incredible connection to the Spirit World and spiritual understanding.

Transcendence: Moving above and beyond the physical experience. Transcendence allows our consciousness to see our life experience from a higher perspective, giving us the ability to rise above it and gaze upon it, rather than feeling stuck in it.

Transformation: Changing from one form to another. We experience this multiple times in our lives as we move through phases of growth. For many, this eventually includes a spiritual transformation as we come to recognize our own spiritual beliefs, essence, and connection, which may not be aligned with the religion we were born into. This transformation process is often depicted as a caterpillar remembering what it truly is and was always meant to be, before emerging into its full glory as a butterfly. We are now in a collective transformation, with humanity moving from its caterpillar phase into the cocoon, as all our systems and perceived reality break down. We will reconstruct ourselves and emerge from our dark cocoon into a new world that is so much more beautiful than we can now presently imagine.

Transhumanism: the theory that humans can physically and mentally evolve through merging technology with biology. This biohacking of the divine human blueprint is sold to humanity in the name of extended life and making the world a better place by becoming less human. Its intent is to cut us off from our true divine nature.

Transmute/Transmutation: Changing fear and darkness into love and light. We can revisit past painful experiences, unresolved issues, and shadow aspects of ourselves that were hidden, expose them, and turn them into learning lessons rather than suffering. This occurs by shining light into our own dark stories and viewing new perceptions through continual application of love in all its forms and functions. This process is also necessary for healing and uplifting the entire human/Earth existence as well, as our own personal experiences, beliefs, and issues.

Tuning In: Listening to Spirit's guidance. A non-religious term for praying and actively listening for answers. This guidance can come from our higher selves, guardian angels, beings of light and God. It is vital to clear your field and set spiritual protection before tuning in to ensure that no lower energies and thoughts can infiltrate the messages you receive. Much like tuning into a radio station, your own vibration, and the vibration you tune into determines the quality of the message.

Tunnel Diggers: Individuals who take the time to research into the dark side and then bring the information up to be spread forward. They follow money trails, lost history, hidden secrets, etc. and are vital to the revelation and revolution.

Unified Field: Where two or more are gathered (not necessarily in person) with a singular focus and conscious intent. In this interconnectedness, miracles, breakthroughs, coincidences, and synchronicities can occur in amazing ways.

Unity Consciousness: The opposite of duality perception. Duality is the belief that one must lose for another to win; also known as the zero-sum game. Duality keeps us stuck in "divide and conquer" mode; there is always an Us vs. Them/Right vs. Wrong scenario. Unity consciousness focuses on what is best for all concerned. There is no win/lose or Us vs. Them... there is only We. Where we go one, we go all—and we are all in this together.

Unresolved Issues: Fear-based beliefs and unconscious programming surrounding past painful experiences that keep us stuck in the present. All of us have fear-based beliefs and painful memories that began in childhood and have replayed themselves in various scenarios throughout our lives, becoming our personal pain stories. These ego and heart wounds must be processed and resolved, in order to learn their lessons and end the story for good. Once we learn how to view and resolve our personal unresolved issues, we can use that same healing process to navigate and heal our collective human story and unresolved issues.

<u>Vesica Piscis / Venn Diagram</u>: A sacred geometry figure consisting of two or three circles of equal size, overlapping each other at the center. In Latin, vesica piscis literally translates to "Vessel of Fish" due to the design's resemblance to a fish. This graphic is an integral part of the Flower of Life, a sacred symbol for all creation, where apparent opposites meet in

harmony with the potential to create something entirely new.

Regarding our present political polarity, with each side represented as a circle, the extreme left and the extreme right are both manipulated by the powers that be for the sole purpose of driving humanity into greater fear, hatred, and division. The 2% on the far extremes are the loudest voices that drive the division and perception of the other 98%. In the center, where both circles overlap, liberals and conservatives actually see eye-to-eye. The more we evolve and open our eyes to all sides of every story, the larger the center of the diagram becomes and those in the middle become the way showers for the rest until the two extremes cease to exist and all that remains is oneness.

Vibrations: See Frequencies.

Walk-In: Advanced souls choosing to replace existing souls which opt-out of the human experience, or advanced souls which choose to work in tandem with existing human souls. There is a soul contract between the advanced soul and the lower soul. The walk-in experience most commonly takes place during a near-death experience.

White Hats: International group of individuals dedicated to penetrating and dismantling the dark agenda. They are part of The Light Alliance which also includes benevolent ETs, Ascended Masters, Angelics and Mother Earth.

Woke: A slang term used in the 1930s referring to an awareness of the social and political issues affecting African Americans. Nearing 2012 it was used by the spiritual community as fun play on words for being spiritually awake. Later the term became politicized and is currently used to divide humanity and keep all sides unable to see the whole picture and unify in full awake and awareness.

Woke Washing: Language intentionally used by organizations, corporations, media, and politics to give people the perception they care about social issues, have morality in mind and genuine intentions that are best for humanity and all life on Earth to illicit our support for their product, service, or movement.

WWGOWGA: Where we go one, we go all. A QAnon hashtag for The Great Awakening. We are all in this together. Stay together, stay one, stay united. No one gets left behind. We are one.

"A house divided against itself cannot stand."

—Abraham Lincoln

Bridging the Divide

In this time of great division, when all factions of humanity have been told to oppose other factions, Patriots and Light Workers have been pitted against each other in the dividing terms of Conservative vs. Liberal. These labels, and the narratives surrounding them, were created to prevent us from unifying. The truth is, the most open-minded people of both camps overlap and meet in the middle of a Venn Diagram. Within the loving center, both sides are warriors fighting for freedom, peace, harmony, prosperity, and all loving aspects of the One Creator (God) on behalf of all humankind. They are far more alike than they are different. The dark powers that be (Cabal) have set them in opposition to each other, knowing if they ever united in one mind and purpose, the rulers at the top would be overthrown.

Those controllers of the planet know all they need to do is say the right words to keep both sides divided and conquered. The powers that be, those who see themselves as better and more deserving than the rest, know how to play the people as pawns in this very complex game of chess. They know how to use just the right words to spin human beings into blind compliance. Yes, free-will-choice is the prime directive on our planet, and they know that if they can word the choices exactly right, people will comply without any real trouble.

For Religious Conservatives all the controllers need to do is add Jesus, God or Allah to their agenda and people blindly follow. They've been doing it for thousands of years. I grew up this way and I've seen firsthand how easily blind faith is manipulated. Too many harms against humanity have been justified in the name of God, using God's name in vain. For the Spiritual Liberals, all the controllers need to do is add Love, Peace and Unity to their agenda and many people blindly follow. Lightworkers want to believe that those in charge want unity, freedom and equality that calls to their own hearts. That desire makes it easy for some of the most loving and light filled individuals to be blinded to the psychological manipulation.

When we strip away what we are being told about each other by outside sources and look only at the mutual purpose of Awakening and Ascension, we can see how powerful we are together, as one. We, united, are a light force to reckon with; together, we will create a new reality based in love, with Divine Love for all life on Earth as our guiding power. Unity will be the primary foundation of our New Earth creation.

"Light and darkness cannot share the same room."

—2 Corinthians 6:14

Light Speed Ahead

A split in realities is well under way. It is a separation of realities where both look identical on the surface yet lead into very different directions. This is what some have termed as a bifurcation of worlds or a two-Earth split. The descending reality is based in fear and control. The ascending reality is based in love and freedom. Those who can raise their vibration to express only light and choose to live only from their hearts, will be a part of the ascending reality.

All Hell is breaking loose, and this is great news! It is breaking loose of its fear tactics and control over humanity. Hell is part of the old world many of us are now choosing to liberate ourselves from. Humanity is in the birth canal between the old world based on fear and the new Earth based on love. We will find the light at the end of the tunnel and rebirth ourselves as beings of light and love in a whole new world.

The New Earth which has been prophesied for thousands of years is upon us and being birthed through each of us as we hold this vision as our collective intent. Once we finish breaking free of the old reality we will have a thousand years of peace, or more, as we choose for our planet to be a planet based solely on love.

There may be many who choose to stay in the fear-based reality because that is where they are comfortable. They like their stressful news, negative television, violent movies, sport conflicts, spiteful division, tracking devices and false sense of security. They are as happy as they know how to be.

Even when made fully aware of the game that is being played on them, they will choose to stay and play that way. Some people feel right at home where they have always been enslaved because the unknown world appears more frightening than the discomfort of their comfort zone. Remember too, that every soul is choosing its human experience and some souls will choose to continue learning through the contrast of fear and darkness.

Others who would prefer the new reality based only on love, harmony, peace, and prosperity, sadly, will not be able to make the jump to light speed. Their physical bodies simply cannot make the alchemical change necessary to exist at the higher vibrational frequencies. And some who believe themselves to be awake and aware will also not be able to make the shift. If they cannot let go of hatred, anger, blame and resentment toward the past they will stay stuck in the past. Once they let down their resistance to change, love will enter their hearts and they can move forward. Again, this involves a soul choice whether to ascend at this time or in another lifetime. Everyone is exactly where their soul chooses for them to be.

Those who are both physically informed and spiritually awakened will lead the way into the new reality, as many already are. The more of us who learn how to consciously lift ourselves up out of fear and into love, and connect with our soul essence, the faster we all can move in our new ascended reality of peace and heaven on Earth. Peace and heaven both begin with finding them within ourselves.

We must each be willing to do the inner work of processing our fear-based beliefs, transmuting our personal pain stories, cleaning up all our judgments, recognizing our individual shadows and dismantling unloving perceptions. We need to let go of our self-righteousness and spiritual arrogance, accepting ourselves and each other in our unique paths and journeys. All this is necessary if we are to create a world of equality, harmony, and prosperity for all.

Love always cancels out fear and light will prevail over darkness. The light always wins, and the darkness is unaware that it is always working on behalf of the light. Light can work wonders under the cover of darkness and as the darkness exposes itself, humanity will emerge into the light. It is light speed ahead!

While there will be some who cannot make the switch to light speed, most will. All it really requires is an open mind, a loving heart, and a genuine desire for a better world. When enough of us choose this, it will become our collective reality and the old reality based on fear will fade away into nothing more than stories of our past. Someday we will look back on this time, and the times that came before, and see these as nothing more than learning lessons from which sprang a whole new world of understanding.

"We ask ourselves, who am I to be brilliant, gorgeous, handsome, talented and fabulous? Actually, who are you not to be?"

—Marianne Williamson

The Returns

One lesson humanity may finally be learning from the past is that waiting to be rescued by an external savior only delays their deliverance from suffering. If we are to create the world seeking to be created through us, it is time to stop waiting to be rescued and become the saviors of ourselves.

Yes, there are individuals who have been seen as heroes throughout the human story and we admire them for their courage and conviction to stand up to those who oppressed them and their people, and showed us an example of what is possible when we stand up for ourselves. They show us what is possible when we band together for change and together change the world. These men and women from history, from Moses to Joan of Arc, and Yeshah (Jesus) to Ghandi, and yes, even Donald Trump, have shown us what is possible when one person steps up and doesn't back down to their oppressors. And, what isn't heralded are the people who shared the load and stood up for themselves.

In 2013, I received a message and vision from The Guardians of Light and Protectors of Earth's Ascension. These are Ascended Masters and Archangels who are working on humanity's behalf in higher dimensions. As I stood outside my house one morning, I saw on my right the etheric image of an elderly Caucasian man and was told he was a man of notoriety and influence. I had the distinct impression he was a television personality but not an actor. At the time I didn't think to ask his name, I was simply surprised he was not a politician.

On my left I saw the etheric image of Hillary Clinton. My walkway divided them. I heard the words, "Between him and Hillary, the corruption will be exposed." At the time, I knew nothing of Hillary's back story, and I expected they would be working together to expose the corruption. Because of my own expectation, I did not see the correlation with my vision when Hillary and Donald Trump went up against each other in the 2016 election, three years later.

When Trump won that election, it was clear to me he had been put into place by The Guardians and that corruption would be exposed because of the role he played in the White House. I did not recognize him as the one in my vision who would expose the corruption. I merely saw, as many did, that his position of authority was a clear indication of how depraved our country had become. I saw him as an embodiment of the corruption and believed his mere presence would cause people to wake up and see how desperately we need to change our systems.

I had known for over ten years, as many in the Spiritual Community have, that all our systems needed to fail in order to be rebuilt. I assumed his presence on the scene would be the beginning of the collapse with his track record of greed, arrogance, and blame. I only saw what the media told me to see and was unaware of how mainstream media was part of the dark agenda to keep humanity under the controls of fear. I didn't see how, "follow the money," a mantra I've used for years to see what is really happening in the world and where greed plays a role, also involved the media.

As with so many other in the spiritual community, I trusted the media and had no reason to distrust them. Sure I was frustrated with their insistence on only showing fear-based stories because fear sells, and news had become little more than tabloid TV, but it never crossed my mind they were intentionally deceitful. I knew about soundbite editing, green screens, photoshopping and beta footage, but didn't think of it in terms of newscasting. I saw Trump as self-grandiose filled with hatred and blame, with no real solutions and only focused on the problems of the past. This is the reason so many in the spiritual community could not see him as a leader chosen on their behalf.

In early 2019, a friend whom I dearly trust, suggested I tune in with an open heart and mind, and listen to Spirit's guidance about the role Trump really plays. I was surprised at what I discovered. What many don't know is that President Trump had an awakening experience in December of 2018 which softened his heart. But the damage had already been done by the media and many Light Workers could not see past the drama that came before

It wasn't easy trying to see him through new eyes. At first, I was resistant to the idea that he had been hand-picked by The Guardians to fill the role as president and a leader for the freedom of humanity. The media portrayed him as the opposite – as a dictator who would take away all the rights and freedoms of the people. I checked in again with the Guardians to help me see what I couldn't see. They confirmed that he had been chosen to be a "bull in the china shop" and I was shown The White House as the place China does its shopping. At the time, I had no idea how true that vision was.

In another tune-in The Guardians called him the "wrecking ball" needed to bring down the structures of corruption. Lastly, toward the end of his term, they called him, "Billy Goat Gruff," the one who puts the monsters in their place and makes the bridge from one side to another passable: dark to light. Every time I tuned in, every message that came through about him was a positive message about the role he was chosen to play. What I had seen during his run for office as a crude, hard-headed and egotistical man was exactly the personality needed to get the work done of prepping our country and the world for reconstruction. His background in real estate demolition and construction was apropos.

He was the elderly man I saw standing opposite of Hillary Clinton all those years ago standing on my sidewalk, the one who would help to expose the corruption. As I came to this clear awareness, I could see that from a spiritual perspective, both souls worked together to begin the collapse of the old game. In the physical perspective, between the two of them—with Clinton on her side and Trump on his, on opposite teams—the game of lies, deception and corruption will be fully exposed.

Whether each of us are supporters of his work or not, we can all agree that his presence as the American President became a trigger for The

Great Awakening. As difficult as it may be for some people to accept, Donald Trump was chosen by The Guardians years ago to help expose the corruption and break down the structures of the old world.

He was shoehorned in as President because humanity needed him to be there. His staunch personality prevented him from giving way to the endless media storm. He understood the money game more than most, he was not afraid to stand up to career politicians and he never backed down and gave in to those who were hell bent on destroying him. His refusal to play the controller's way and his unconventional style made him an enemy of the status quo.

Trump remained in his leadership role for as long as was necessary to get the job done in the public eye. Any role he plays from the sidelines needs to remain hidden for greater exposure of corruption to take place. If he were in office as American President while military tribunals occur and treachery exposed, the world would see him as another dictator who destroys his enemies in the pursuit of totalitarianism.

While Trump may be playing a role behind the scenes, assisting with exposure of the corruption, and in the necessary break down of old systems, he is not the who many seem to believe him to be. He is not king of the world, and he is not Jesus or God reincarnated. Those who worship him need to stop with the hero worship and their waiting with bated breath for his return. This waiting game serves no one except those who profit from human beings while the wait for someone else to fix the issues at hand. The creators of the issues thrive on our waiting and wishful thinking.

Trump is one of many leaders, one who volunteered for a difficult job, but he is not a savior. He is just one man doing the work he came to Earth to do. He is a human being with all the fallibilities of being human. His entrance on the political scene was a catalyst for massive change. His stormy presidency and his standing up to the swamp monsters in what some see as dignity rather than arrogance, ignited many individuals to recognize what is possible and what exists within each one of us.

While the dark side used and continues to use Trump's presence on the scene to further divide us, many began recognizing the intentional division and how humanity has been used in a game of divide and conquer. In this awareness they became even more united in the light. All over the world humanity began to unify under the banner of freedom.

Now with President Trump no longer in the forefront, many are still waiting for his return. They are waiting for a savior to rescue them and in their waiting and wanting, without action or movement, they wait. They've been waiting for thousands of years for an external savior to rescue them and wonder why nothing really changes. Waiting around to be rescued sends a clear message to the universe that we are not ready to change our circumstances. This is not unlike an abused wife who waits for her husband to change, or waits for someone to see her trauma, break into her home, and rescue her.

The rescuing always has to come from within ourselves and our willingness to change our circumstances. When we do, when we stop waiting for Trump, Jesus, Nesara, Solar Flash, new politicians or anything else to rescue us, and stand up for ourselves, then the world we seek will come as an energetic match to what we put out. When we refuse to be couch potatoes hoping to be rescued while not bothering to help ourselves, then we will experience the divine intervention we seek. We've got to stop waiting for a man in a white house or a man on a white horse to rescue us, and instead, become the rescuers.

What many don't understand is that the return of the physical embodiment of Jesus will occur when enough of humanity has already lifted themselves up and stop waiting for his return.

The Christ has already returned through each of us who raise our vibration to the consciousness of pure, unconditional love. This is the Christ consciousness being returned and resurrected through each of us. The foretold second coming of Christ and the resurrection are already well in process. The ascension began in the early 1960s when love began returning to the planet and those in fear became desperate to retain control.

The story of Jesus returning and waiting for him to save humanity was created and interpreted by the dark side to keep human beings from finding their true inner power and their own inner light. It was created to keep people waiting to be rescued, rather than rescuing themselves, while the dark side went about their business.

It was created to prevent humanity from finding its oneness and direct connection to Divine Love and Divine Light which exists within each of us. It was created to keep us from discovering who we really are and what we are fully capable of as divine souls having a human experience. It was created to prevent humanity from unifying and seeing how they have been played.

At the core, all religions are based on the universal truths of love, peace, and harmony while surrounding dogma keeps them in fear and prevents them from finding their true inner essence and direct connection to The Divine. These are fear-based beliefs disguised as love and have been used for millennia by the dark side of the contrast to keep humanity under control.

The second coming of Christ is the return of Christ Consciousness, the consciousness of unconditional love and the spirit of freedom now making waves across the planet and is held within each one of our hearts. The foretold resurrection is the resurrection of the Divine Feminine. It is the return of The Mother and Her loving compassion for all creation. Her love, Her heart, Her compassion is what has been missing from the human experience. In Her love, we are all lifted to new heights of love and compassion for each other.

We are all the apocalypse, ascension, second coming, and resurrection. We are restoring our hearts and remembering who we are. We are the ones we've been waiting for, and we are the ones who will save humanity through the love, light, and truth we espouse. We are all leaders of the evolution, and it is time for us to stop looking for others to lead us and find the leader within. We have all been Christed and each of us is chosen to help lead the way for humanity to create a new reality.

We are Light Workers, not Light waiters, and it is time for us to get to work. Yes, be the light and be the love, and also be in inspired action. We attract what we are and what we do. The Law of Attraction is always working, and we attract what we put out. The more gratitude we feel in our hearts the more we are given to be grateful for, and half of the word attraction is action, so what we act upon is necessary for manifestation.

Sitting in love and light, waiting and wanting does assist the energetic process and can attract resources and synchronicities but does not speed the process of creation. Our divinely guided actions create our reality. It's time for each of us to recognize the role we play in the creation process and choose to be responsible for the roles we play, have played in the past, and will play moving forward.

Remember, God/Source/Universe/Spirit/Love… by whatever name you most align, helps those who help themselves and matches what we put forward. We show our intent through our thoughts, feelings, voices, choices and actions. Our vibrational resonance causes the universe and life to match our energy, and our action prompts the energy to action.

Spirit meets us at the point of action and assists our forward focused intent. Let our thoughts, feelings, emotions, and action be forward action always in what we want to see the world become, rather than opposing what has always been. Let us all remain focused on, "what am I working toward and for?" rather than, "what am I fighting against?" Imagine the world you want to create, then put your heart into the work of creating it. This is where all of us, across all divides, will now unify in plan and purpose. One purpose, one love, for all life on Earth.

That is how we change the world, that is how we find peace for all and heaven on earth. It's in every one of us just waiting for us to find it and grow it within ourselves. Heaven really is at hand, in our hands, and waiting for us to manifest it into our individual and collective reality. As within, so without, as below so above. It's in us, it has always been in us, simply waiting for us to rise to our own occasion.

"The purpose of human life is to serve, and to show compassion and the will to help others."

—Albert Schweitzer

All for One

We are amid one of the greatest and most rare events ever to occur in the known Universe. Both our planet and her people are ascending into higher frequencies at the same time. The entire universe is watching to see how it is done. This moment in our concept of time will cause humanity to rise to its full potential and inspire the entire universe to what is possible.

The awakening and remembering of who we are is a team effort. Those who have awakened first, both with awareness of physical information and are spiritually awake, are destined to help the rest of humanity navigate the pain that comes with all breakdowns. All breakthroughs into the light stems from breaking down old perceptions.

All Earthlings are being invited to ascend into the new loving reality rather than only the chosen few. All who can raise their vibration into love and light will be ascending into the new world, as we, those who have already awakened and processed our personal beliefs into higher understanding, prepare the place for them. Where we go one, we go all. No one gets left behind except by their conscious choice. Conscious choice is on the horizon.

As creators of our reality, inter-creators with each other and co-creators with Source/God, we collectively choose when we are finished with learning through suffering. We choose when we are finished with the dark contrast we have labeled as evil. We collectively choose when we are complete and no longer allow fear to control our outcomes and physical experiences. As one human body, as a collective of souls, we have chosen for Earth to no longer be a learning planet and now choose to make it a place of peace and a respite for the souls which incarnate here. On a soul level this choice has already been made. We need now only choose it as a collective physical choice and it will be done. It is already written in the stars, and we need only agree for it to be our reality.

We have the hindsight to see what has happened in the past and recognition of what is occurring in the present, and we are the visionaries who will create a new reality. As darkness and dis-ease are brought forward, we are collapsing all systems and structures we have collectively outgrown. We are now given the opportunity to create new concepts and structures that serve all of humanity—systems that support all life on Earth. All fear, deception and corruption are presently being brought to the surface, swept out from under rugs and skeletons pulled from closets for our acknowledgement and conscious resolution. These dark remnants of the human experience are being brought forward for us to process and put behind us. We cannot take our baggage with us into the new world we are inter-creating.

Much of humanity has finally come to accept and understand that WE are the change we want to see in the world. We are beginning to fully understand what, "if it is to be, it is up to me," really means, and now fully understanding that "if it is to be, it is up to WE." We are finally embodying "we're the ones we've been waiting for" and seeing how "we the people" have the real power. We are starting to see how our collective consciousness and the choices we have made created the mess we are presently in. We also now see how our collective consciousness and the choices we make moving forward will create the new world.

God helps those who help themselves and it is up to us to step up. The Universe is always working on our behalf and provides us with what we focus on. The more we focus on lack and brokenness, the more we receive the same. When we focus on problems, we get more problems. This also holds true with focusing on what we want to see in the world.

We need to first shift our focus, and create from what we want, rather than from what we don't want. We can blame this present reality on Satan, his followers and his minions or any other purveyor of what has been labeled as evil. We can continue waiting for Jesus to come and rescue us as our ancestors before us did, and as we wait our reality continues to go downhill. Or we can accept responsibility for the truth that we have collectively created our reality and we will collectively re-create it.

We are made in the likeness and image of God, and as such, we are creators. We have created our reality and we have within us the ability to create it anew. We are all creators, and we are all divine intervention. We are all one with God and God works through each of us. All of us are the re-creators that will step forward and design our new reality. We will create the new constructs which will be put into place for an entirely new human experience. Anything we can imagine is possible, because with God, with love, all things are possible. Divine Love, through each of us, makes all things new.

Rather than focusing on the problems and complaining about what has not worked, let us get to work focusing on solutions. The reason we are in the mess we are in is because we've been waiting for someone else to clean up after us, do the work for us, rescue us, and make our decisions for us. Blame, resentment, and victimization only disempower us and slow our progression into a better world. It's time to step up our game.

The time of follow the leader is over. That is part of the old-world paradigm. The new world we are creating, as the old-world crumbles, is based in co-operation and mutual support. It is based on unification rather than separation. It is based in service to the whole, rather than service to self. It is based in love and leads from the heart, rather than controlled by fear and ego. It is understanding that every person has a role to play, and every role is an equally necessary part of moving us forward into the existence we desire to create.

The world around us is always a reflection of our inner world. If we want to save the world, we must first save ourselves from the darkness within. We are not the savior of others. When we have found light within ourselves we light the way for others to save themselves. When enough of us do the inner work, it extends into the world around us, and when enough of humanity has done the inner work to find peace within themselves, then we will have the paradise we seek.

Have faith in humanity, have faith in yourself and let the light of living love guide you forward. Together we will envision and create a new reality, the new golden age of humanity, where all flourishes in peace and prosperity. Yes, I really do think this is possible; it just needs enough of us to believe it is and be willing to see it for all of us. It needs enough of us to see through the eyes of neutrality and begin loving affirmative action.

Utopia, where all of life thrives, is possible when enough of us hold it in our vision, feel it in our hearts, lock arms together, do the work and march forward into the light. We are one family, and this is our home. It is time for us to step up, rise, and make our home the way WE, all the children of Earth, all life on Earth want and deserve for it to be.

About the Author

Victoria Reynolds is a Spiritual Luminary, Oracle of Freedom, and Broadcaster. Her role on the planet is to assist humanity in processing the past, breaking free from the controls of fear-based beliefs, and to rise into a new reality based on love. Victoria experienced her mid-life awakening following the 2008 recession and began teaching others what her higher-self, spirit guides, ascended guardians and God teach to her. To learn more about Victoria, visit victoriareynolds.com.

Made in the USA
Las Vegas, NV
06 April 2023